A long time ago, as a
Little girl, I dreamed
Of traveling all over
The world.

And often I'd ask
About the past
Driving everyone
Crazy fast!

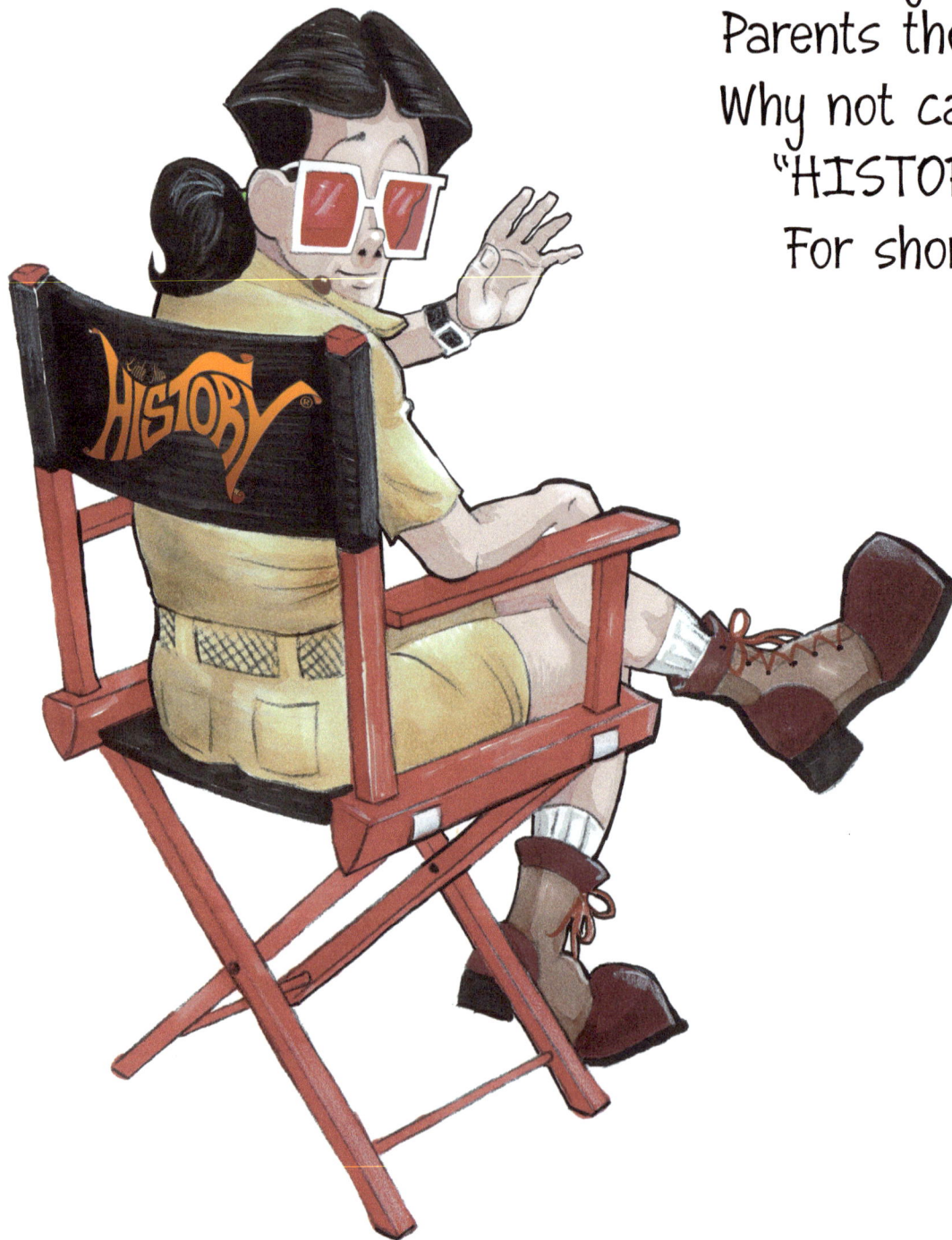

Amused by this my
Parents thought,
Why not call me
"HISTORY"
For short?

Since then I've traveled by
Land, sea, and air...

3

...So read this book
And I'll take you
Somewhere!

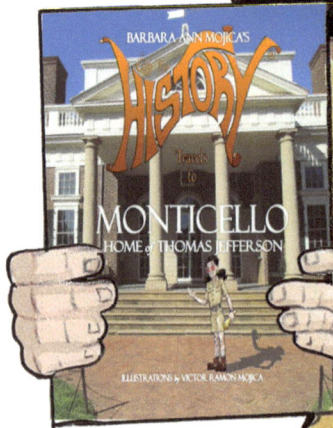

Little Miss HISTORY Travels to MONTICELLO
Home *of* Thomas Jefferson
© 2022 Barbara Ann Mojica. All Rights Reserved.

Published in The UNITED STATES of AMERICA
eugenus STUDIOS, LLC
P.O. BOX 213
Valatie, NY 12184
E-Mail: Barbara@LittleMissHISTORY.com
WebSite: www.LittleMissHISTORY.com

ISBN-13: 978-1-7330671-8-8

Dedicated to Thomas Jefferson's

Descendants

BARBARA ANN MOJICA'S

Little Miss

HISTORY®

Travels to

MONTICELLO
HOME *of* THOMAS JEFFERSON

Illustrations by VICTOR RAMON MOJICA

Enter the world of Thomas Jefferson, president, philosopher, scientist, architect, and author of The Declaration of Independence.

He was born on his father's Shadwell plantation along the Rivanna River in the foothills of the Blue Ridge Mountains in central Virginia.

Peter Jefferson, his father, was a planter and surveyor.
His mother, Jane Randolph, came from a wealthy family.

Jefferson dreamed about living on the mountain he played on as a boy. In 1768, he began clearing that site.

The name Monticello means "little mountain." Jefferson designed the house in the neoclassical style...

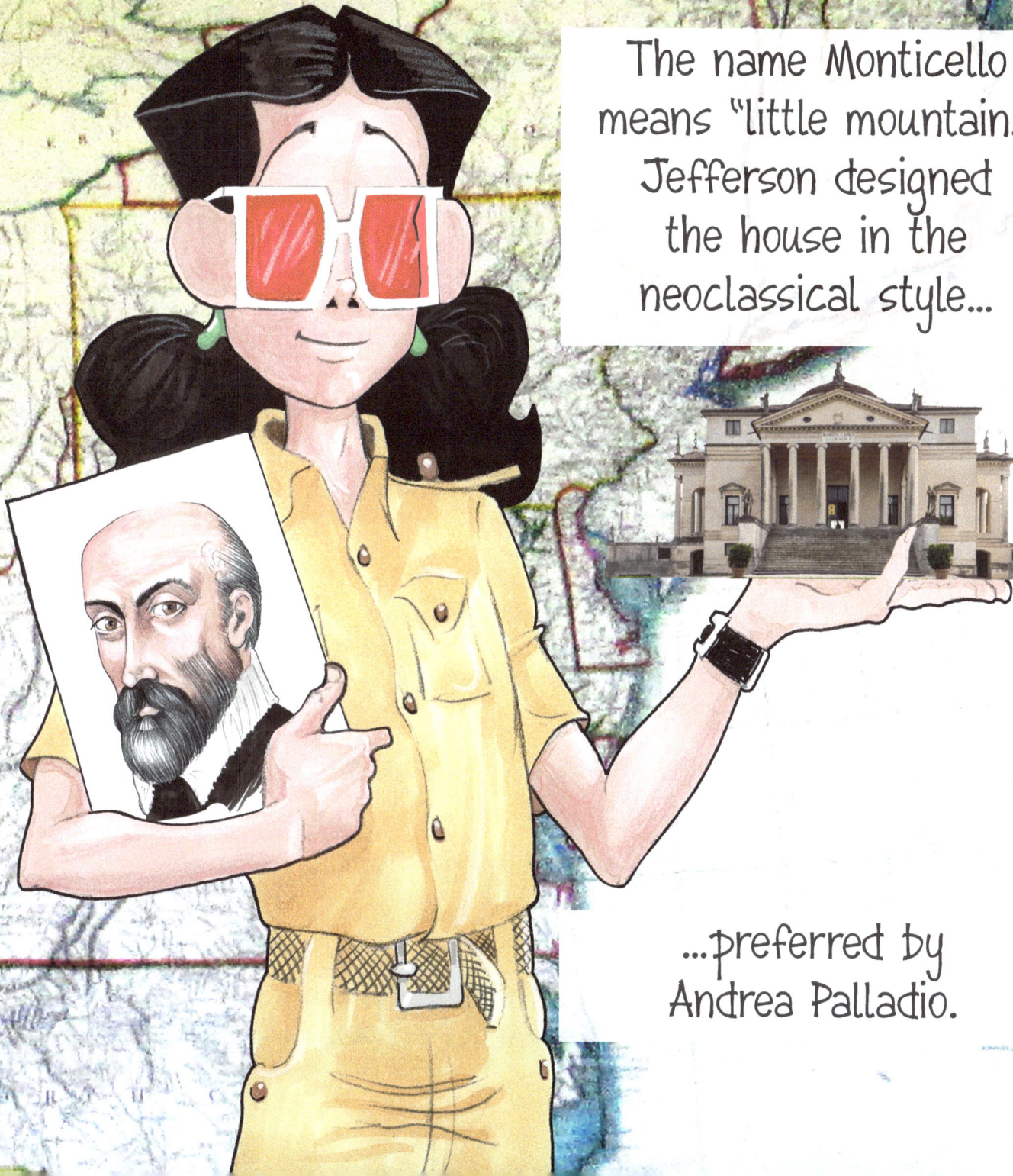

...preferred by Andrea Palladio.

The first version was a two-story, eight-room house on a plantation of 5,000 acres.

Jefferson moved into The South Pavilion in 1770.

Two years later, his new wife
Martha Wayles Skelton joined him.

THOMAS JEFFERSON

13 AVRIL 1743
À SHADWELL
EN VIRGINIE

4 JUILLET 1826
À MONTICELLO
EN VIRGINIE

SYMBOLE DE L'AMITIÉ FRANCO-AMÉRICAINE

AMBASSADEUR DES ETATS-UNIS EN FRANCE 1785-1789
3ᵐᵉ PRÉSIDENT DES ETATS-UNIS 1801-1809
AUTEUR PRINCIPAL DE LA RÉDACTION DE L'INDÉPENDANCE AMÉRICAINE
4 JUILLET 1776. AMOUREUX DE LA FRANCE, IL VOYAGE, PARCOURT NOS
TERRITOIRES ET PROMEUT AUX ETATS-UNIS NOTRE PATRIMOINE - ARCHITECTURE,
TERROIRS, CULTURE. HUMANISTE, IL PARTAGE NOS VALEURS DE LIBERTÉ. AVEC SON
AMI LA FAYETTE, IL JOUE UN RÔLE CLÉ DANS L'ÉBAUCHE DE LA CONSTITUTION
FRANÇAISE ET DE LA DÉCLARATION DES DROITS DE L'HOMME ET DU CITOYEN

Soon after Martha died in 1782, Jefferson left America to become Minister to France.
After returning, he began transforming Monticello into his three-story twenty-one-room brick "essay in architecture."

FONDERIES DECHAUMONT À MURET

Jefferson added a center hallway and a set of rooms on both sides, more than doubling its area. He removed the second story and replaced it with a mezzanine bedroom floor.

The design focused on two large rooms used as an entrance hall and museum set up to impress visitors.

Here Jefferson displayed his scientific instruments and a music sitting room.

The Great Clock he designed contained heavy weights that drop to the floor and mark the day of the week as they descend through the floor. The markers for Friday and Saturday are in the cellar.

Curiosities brought back by Lewis and Clark's exploration of land that would become the Louisiana Purchase and Native-American artifacts decorated the walls. Jefferson included busts of Roman art, maps, and paintings.

Jefferson rarely used this room because it was either too hot or cold and only reachable by a flight of stairs that were narrow and steep.

Jefferson's granddaughters used a
small storage room within nicknamed "The Cuddy"
as their private meeting place.

The south wing includes Jefferson's private rooms. Jefferson believed in efficiency. He built beds into alcoves that contained storage to save space.

Jefferson's bed opened to two sides, one to his study and the other to his bedroom.

His first library burned. Jefferson sold his second library in 1815 to the United States Congress to replace the books lost when the British burned Washington in 1814.

Today, The Library of Congress is the largest library in the world, with millions of books, recordings, photographs, newspapers, maps, and manuscripts in its collections. The Library is the main research arm of the U.S. Congress and the home of the U.S. Copyright Office.

The north wing included two guest bedrooms and an efficient dining room. Dumbwaiters and elevators built on sides of the fireplace lifted wine from the cellars.

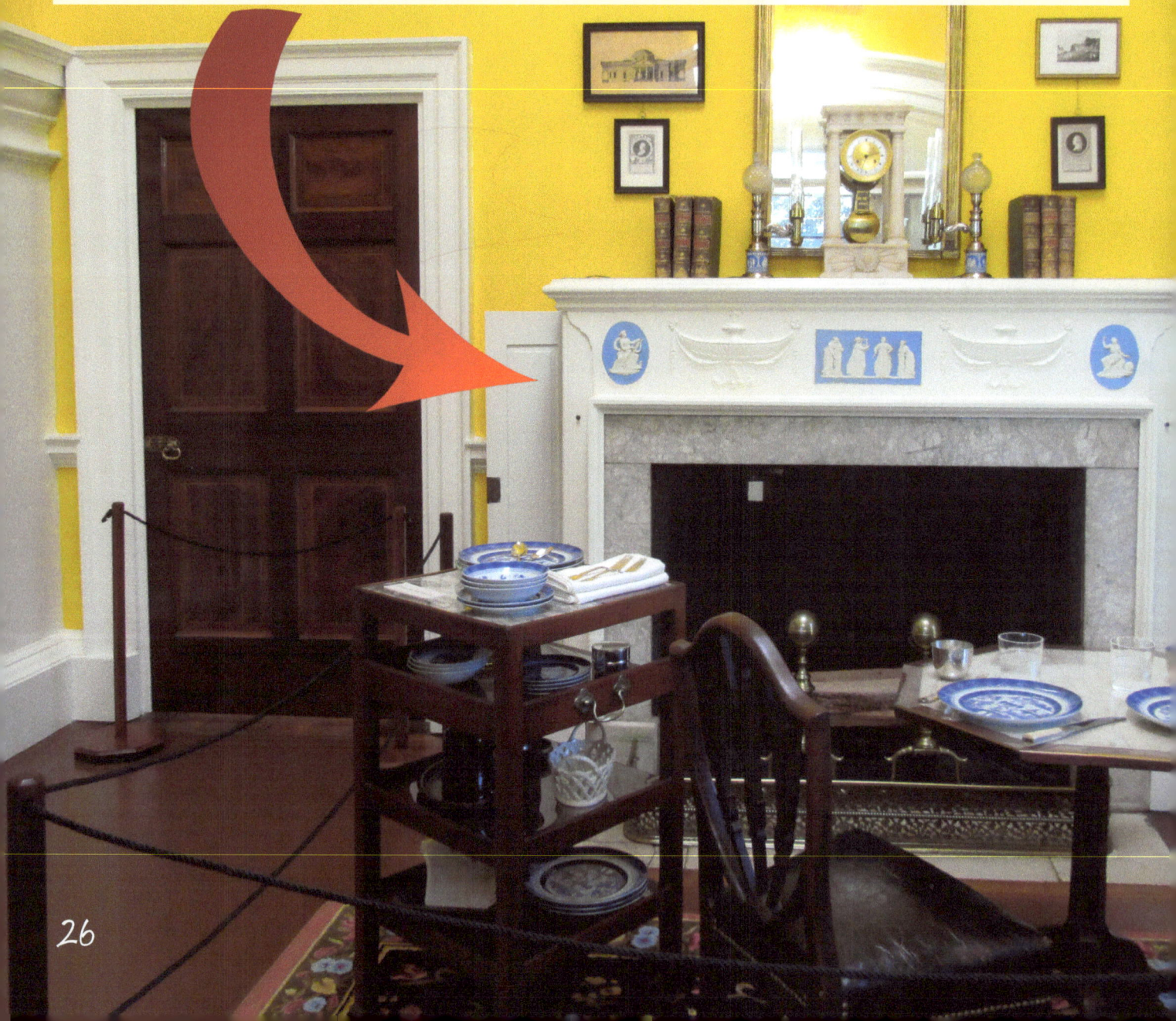

Servants carried food platters in hidden hallways to the kitchens from the dining room.

Tables remained folded until mealtimes.

Who lived at Monticello besides Jefferson, and what did they do?

Jefferson used enslaved African people
to grow tobacco and food,
later shifting from tobacco to wheat.

A row of outbuildings contained a dairy, a washhouse, storehouses, a small nail factory, and joinery to make furniture. A stone weaver's cottage and the tall chimney of the joinery survive. Mulberry Row is now an archeological site to learn more about enslaved people at the plantation.

Moses Gillette, Jr.
Gillette descendant

Families lived
in slavery at
Monticello
for three
or more
generations.

FOSSETT FAMILY

From the age of twelve, Joseph Fossett was separated from his mother, Mary Hemings Bell, who lived as a free person in Charlottesville, the common-law wife of white merchant Thomas Bell. Fossett remained in slavery at Monticello, where he became head blacksmith. He and his wife, Edith Hern Fossett, endured a six-year separation while she learned French cooking and served President Jefferson in Washington. After Jefferson's death in 1826, Fossett was one of five slaves freed in his will, but his wife and seven of their children were auctioned to different bidders. Fossett opened a blacksmith's shop in Charlottesville and labored for ten years to buy the freedom of his family. They reunited in Ohio.

GILLETTE FAMILY

Edward and Jane Gillette were farm laborers on the Monticello plantation. Their 12 children became coopers (barrel makers), cooks, shoemakers, and grooms for Jefferson's horses. Jefferson paid Barnaby Gillette to maximize his production of flour barrels. Other family members earned money by selling fish, produce, chickens, and eggs to the Jefferson family. Israel Gillette remembered Jefferson's death in 1826 as "an affair of great moment and uncertainty." Months later, three generations of Gillettes—23 people, including Moses Gillette, who worked as a cooper—were sold at auction. The receipt for Moses Gillette recorded his purchase price of $545.

HEMINGS FAMILY

Elizabeth Hemings, the daughter of an African woman and a white man, headed a large family at Monticello that included 80 people, spanning five generations. The Hemingses were connected to Jefferson's family by blood. Jefferson inherited the family from his father-in-law, John Wayles, who fathered six of Elizabeth Hemings's 12 offspring, making them half-siblings of Jefferson's wife Martha. They enjoyed favored status at Monticello—most of them worked as craftsmen and house servants. John Hemings (his spelling) was a woodworker; James Hemings, a chef; and Peter Hemings, a cook and brewer. In the next generation, Wormley Hughes was the head gardener and cared for the horses, and Burwell Colbert was Monticello's butler and Jefferson's valet. Sally Hemings had at least six children with Thomas Jefferson, four of whom lived to adulthood. Of the more than 600 individuals Jefferson owned, he freed ten, all members of the Hemings family, including his mixed-race children with Sally Hemings.

Elizabeth Hemings and her children arrived at Monticello around 1774 as part of Jefferson's inheritance from his father-in-law, John Wayles.

They helped build the Monticello house, ran the household, made furniture, cooked Jefferson's meals, cared for his children and grandchildren, attended to him in his last moments and dug his grave.

Isaac (Granger) Jefferson
Granger descendant

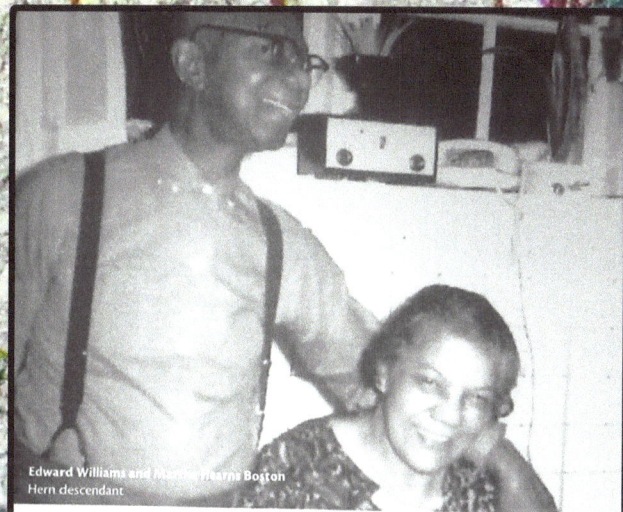

Edward Williams and Martha Hearns Boston
Hern descendant

For 25 years, the Grangers were crucial to Monticello's operation. Ursula Granger supervised cooking, brewing, and the laundry. Her husband George became the plantation's only enslaved overseer. They had three sons: Bagwell, a farm laborer, and George, Jr. and Isaac, both blacksmiths. Ursula, George, and George, Jr. died

GRANGER FAMILY

within months of one another in 1799-1800, after an illness and treatment from an African American healer. Bagwell and his wife were sold at auction after Jefferson's death in 1826. Jefferson gave Isaac Granger, his wife and children, to daughter Maria upon her marriage in 1797. Isaac Granger eventually gained his freedom and added the surname Jefferson, although the details of his arrangement are unknown. In the 1840s, he recounted his memories of life at Monticello to a minister. His memoir is a rare firsthand account of slavery in the United States.

Even though slave marriages were not legally recognized in Virginia, some Monticello families forged lasting unions. David and Isabel Hern's at least 30-year marriage produced 12 children. The Hern family raised Jefferson's crops, drove his wagons, cooked his meals, forged iron, repaired farm equipment, and blasted rock for a canal.

HERN FAMILY

Edith Hern Fossett, a daughter of David and Isabel Hern, became one of Monticello's head cooks after learning French cookery in the President's House in Washington. When Moses and James Hern married women owned by different slaveholders, they persuaded Jefferson to purchase and unite their families. Still, after Jefferson's death, the auction separated 34 members of the Hern family.

Sally Hemings, an enslaved person, was likely the mother to four of Jefferson's children.

We don't know what Sally looked like, but she was described as "light colored and decidedly good looking" with long straight hair down her back."

Those freed legally from the Jefferson household came from the Hemings family.

Jefferson hired a series of white joiners, including James Dinsmore and John Neilson. They trained slave apprentices like John Hemmings, who crafted Monticello's woodwork.

James Dinsmore

John Neilson

In 1993, Monticello historians began an oral history project between Monticello and the Smithsonian National Museum of African American History and Culture called "Getting Word."

The Getting Word Oral History Project

By interviewing descendants of Monticello's enslaved families, they hoped to capture their ancestor's words.

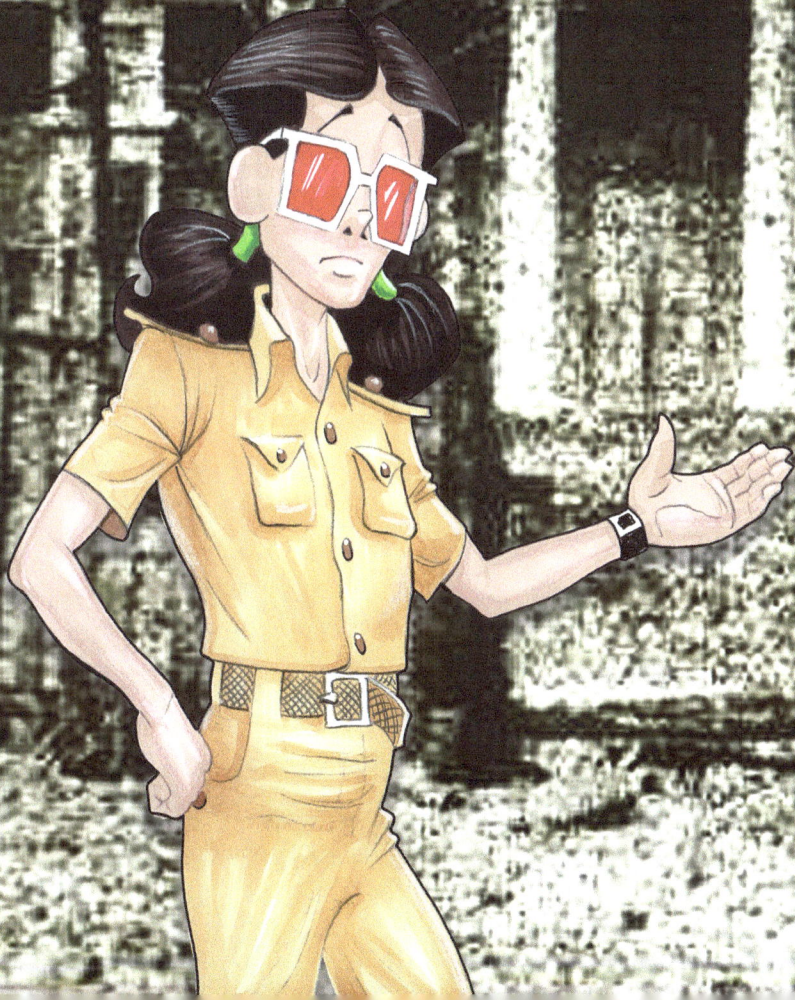

What happened to Monticello
after Thomas Jefferson died?

When Jefferson died on July 4, 1826, he left a debt of $107,000, over a million dollars in today's money.

His daughter, Martha Jefferson Randolph, sold the land, house, and household contents, including 130 enslaved men, women, and children, to satisfy that debt.

In 1834, it was bought by Uriah P. Levy, a commodore in the U.S. Navy, who admired Jefferson and spent his own money to preserve the property.

His nephew Jefferson Monroe Levy took over the property in 1879 and invested considerable money to restore and preserve it. In 1923, Monroe Levy sold it to the Thomas Jefferson Foundation, which now operates the house as a museum and educational institution.

The Monticello Association owns the cemetery,
a society of his descendants through his wife
Martha Wayles Skelton Jefferson.

GLOSSARY FOR MONTICELLO

Alcove – a small part of a room set back from the rest

Architecture – the science or art of designing buildings

Artifacts – objects made or shaped by human hands

Dumbwaiters – small elevators to move food from one place to another

Curiosities – unusual or strange objects

Enslaved – a person who is owned by another and forced to work without pay or rights

Joiner – a person who makes woodwork used in buildings like doors and window frames or furniture

Mezzanine – a smaller floor between two main floors, sometimes serving as a balcony

Neoclassical – a building style based on ancient Roman and Greek designs

Octagon – an eight sided shape

Oral history – learning about past from the spoken stories

Pavilion – a building with open sides used for shelter or recreation

Philosopher – a person who studies the nature of life, truth, and knowledge

Portico – a covered walkway with a roof held up by columns

Surveyor – a person whose job is to measure the boundaries of land

THOMAS JEFFERSON POLITICAL CAREER

1768 elected to the House of Burgesses in Virginia

1775 elected to The Continental Congress

1776 appointed to revise Virginia's laws

1776 drafted The Declaration of Independence

1777 drafted Virginia statute of religious freedom

1779-81 Served as Governor of Virginia

1780 began his book, "Notes on the State of Virginia"

1784-89 Served as US Minister to France

1790-93 Served as the first Secretary of State

1797-1801 Served as the second Vice President under John Adams

1801-09 Served as the third US President

POINTS TO PONDER... WHAT DID YOU LEARN?

1. When and where was Thomas Jefferson born?

2. Name five accomplishments.

3. Who lived and worked at Monticello?

4. What famous document did Jefferson write?

5. What other political offices did he hold?

6. Why do you think Jefferson owned slaves while ending the slave trade?

7. Tell about your favorite parts of Monticello.

8. Describe daily life at Monticello.

9. What were some of Jefferson's greatest achievements?

10. What were some of his weaknesses?

11. What part of Jefferson's collection impresses you most?

12. If you lived at Monticello, what job would you like to have and why?

13. Do you agree it is important to record the words of our ancestors?

14. One needs to study history to understand why things happened and how we got to where we are today. Is that statement true or false?

15. Can one judge the actions of people in the past by today's standards?

16. Can we use what we learn from history to improve and change what will happen in the future? Explain your answer.

BARBARA ANN MOJICA's

NEXT STOP...

Little Miss

HISTORY ®

Travels to

USS SLATER
Destroyer Escort

Illustrations by VICTOR RAMON MOJICA

www.ingramcontent.com/pod-product-compliance
Lightning Source LLC
Chambersburg PA
CBHW042059040426
42448CB00002B/65